Evelyn's

Amazing Encounters

NURSE GLORIOUS

———————

E. L. Harden

Evelyn's Amazing Encounters: Nurse Glorious

E. L. Harden

Published by DSC Publishers, Inc.

ISBN: 979-8-9985264-6-6

Printed in the USA by E.L. Harden

Table of Contents

Dedication

This book is dedicated to all of those going through any stage of kidney failure, God bless you.

To the caretakers, family and friends who encourage and support the patients, God bless you.

And a big thank you to all the doctors, nurses, CNAs and technicians who looks after those on that difficult road to and through the transplant process, God bless you.

Regardless of the road you walk in life, always make sure you:

Give thanks to the Lord Jesus Christ for His Goodness and Mercy, Amen.

Introduction

Evelyn is a CNA (Certified Nursing Assistant) at Central Hospital in Miami, FL.

She can be described as a true believer in the Lord Jesus Christ and a beacon of hope to the people she encounters at work as a CNA.

Tenitha is her recent encounter at Central Hospital and their bond is instant.

The things they both go through at the hospital can be considered as normal for both CNA's and dialysis patients. I do not discount the difficult encounters both have at times.

This story is fictional but some things in it actually happened to a dear loved one.

It was supernatural back then and even now, as I recount the events that happened.

So, this encounter tells of Evelyn's Journey as a CNA, The Miracle of Nurse Glorious, The Kidney Transplant Journey of Tenitha and The Power of Faith and Friendship.

I hope you enjoy this easy read and may it encourage you to look for hidden gems, great or small, in your walk in life with the Lord Jesus Christ.

Chapter One

THE MEETING

While Evelyn settled into her CNA job at Central Hospital in Miami, Florida, she had a few regular patients who would come in from time to time because they had trouble with their ports.

Tenitha is one of the regular patients she met in the hospital. She is a hemodialysis patient that came to the hospital twice in Evelyn's first week there.

Evelyn felt really bad because Tenitha was trying to get a dialysis port under her skin, but her circulation wasn't strong enough to support that.

As Evelyn started her shift today, she rounded the corner to the first of many rooms, and she paused.

"Oh, wow", she said softly, "Tenitha is here again."

She was sleeping quietly, and Evelyn didn't want to wake her up, but according to the chart, her vitals were needed.

Carefully, she rubbed her arm.

"You're here again."

"Hey, Sis! You can't get rid of me for too long. This place is like my second home!"

From the notations on her chart, she came in just after Evelyn clocked out on Friday, and here it is Monday morning.

Tanitha said, "When you get some time, come back by, I have a story to tell you that you won't believe".

"Alright", Evelyn said. As she finished up her vitals, she said, "See you about noon, we can eat our lunch together".

"Cool," Tenitha said.

For a woman going through all these problems, she was always upbeat.

Chapter Two

THE MIRACLE

At noon, Evelyn brought her lunch bag into Tenitha's room. She was already eating her small portion of lunch.

"They never give you enough food in here," Tenitha said, rolling her eyes. "Let me stop complaining and tell you what happened last night".

"The hospital must have admitted a lot of patients on Saturday night because none of the nurses or CNA's would stop for one minute to bring me what I needed. I knocked my dinner tray over, and one nurse said she would bring me another, but never did. Later, one nurse brought me some crackers, but never brought the soda she promised. Then I was in so much pain, I cried myself to sleep last night, praying to God about everything that was not happening for me. It seemed no one had time or wanted to help me."

"It was maybe 2 am when a soft touch woke me up. I never saw her before. The lighting was low, and I didn't see her face, but I surely saw her name tag that read 'Glorious'. She said, 'Hey baby, how you doing?' By her voice, I could tell she was an older nurse. Her question shocked me because no one else seemed to have time to ask me this in the two days I've been here. So, I told her how I really felt, what happened over the past day and a half, and all the while, she patted my arm and acknowledged that she was listening to everything I was saying. When I was done, I was close to tears. She squeezed my hand and told me, 'I'm so sorry these nurses are not meeting your needs, but I promise you that will change.'

"In my mind, I'm saying, 'yeah, right. I've heard that before.' So, Nurse Glorious told me don't worry about a thing, and to get some rest, and she left the room as quietly as she entered. Not even 5 minutes later, another nurse came in to draw blood. I told her Nurse Glorious just left the room. And she said, 'Nurse who? We don't have anyone here by that name, you must be mistaken.' I told her I saw her name tag, she's older with glasses, lots of curly gray hair, but I didn't see her face. But as that nurse finished taking my blood, she said no one on shift tonight matches that description.

"So, nurses came and went, and no one ever heard of a nurse by the name of Glorious. "One of the older nurses remembered someone by that name years ago, but she retired and even doubted she would still be alive to this day!"

"But get this," Tenitha said, "every nurse I spoke to since Nurse Glorious has been very attentive to my needs, as soon as one leaves, another one stops by to ask if I needed anything!"

Evelyn could hardly believe this story!

Back in Seattle, she heard similar stories from different patients, and they all had a visit from 'Nurse Glorious', but she kept that to herself for now.

"Wow," Evelyn said, "Do you realize what really happened to you? Who really visited you?!"

"Yes," Tenitha sobbed, "I do know. God is Good!"

"All the time," Evelyn said, "all the time!"

Seeing how late it was getting, Evelyn asked Tenitha to exchange phone numbers so they could keep in touch.

Evelyn gave Tenitha a quick hug and told her she was glad she shared with her, and

was excited to extend their friendship outside of this hospital building.

Evelyn knew the odds of a successful kidney transplant would be greater if the donor was alive.

That Small Voice in her mind and heart urged her to see if she could be a blessing to Tenitha.

So, Evelyn secretly had the test done to see if she was a match with Tenitha.

Evelyn was surprised the results came back so quickly. She hurried to Tenitha's room to give her the good news.

Chapter Three

THE SURGERY

When Evelyn arrived at Tenitha's room, they were prepping the room for someone else.

She was really glad they exchanged phone numbers!

So, Evelyn dialed Tenitha's number, but another female answered, saying, "This is Tenitha's number, how can I help you?"

"Can I speak to her?" Evelyn asked.

"Are you her family?"

"No, just a friend."

"I'm sorry, but I can only give information to those on the list. Can you tell me your name?"

"Evelyn."

"So, you are on the list. I'm Susan, the nurse who will be in charge of Tenitha once she gets out of surgery. She was transferred to the transplant unit because she was a match for a donated kidney. She's in surgery right now, and she will call you back when she can. I will let her know you called."

"Oh wow!! Thank you for sharing. I will be praying for Tenitha!"

Susan said, "you're welcome" and hung up the phone.

Evelyn found a quiet corner in the break room and began to lift up a prayer for Tenitha.

She then texted some of her close friends from church and asked them to pray for Tenitha also.

Evelyn decided not to say anything to Tenitha about the test results yet.

The next day, Evelyn stopped by Tenitha's room before starting her shift.

There she was, sitting in a chair watching TV. Somehow, she looked a lot younger now.

Lost in thought, she heard Tenitha saying, "Earth to Evelyn, hello?"

"I'm so sorry, you caught me staring at you. I can't believe how different you look!!"

Tenitha said, "Let me tell you how different I feel!! I feel like I could run down the hall and back without breaking a sweat!"

"That's awesome!" Evelyn said.

"Do you mind if I ask you a personal question?"

"Girlie, you can ask me anything."

"OK, but don't be mad at what I'm about to say. When I first met you, you looked like you were at least 50 years old. But today, you don't look a day over thirty! Please tell me how old you are, and I want the truth!"

Tenitha started laughing but stopped short.

"Ouch!! Those stitches really hurt when I laugh! If you must know, I'm 35 and I'll be 36 on May 22nd. And I know what you mean. When I looked in the mirror, I thought I was sent back in time. Having kidney failure really takes a toll on the body."

"Wow, I can see the difference!" Evelyn said aloud.

"I need to start my shift. How long are they keeping you in here?"

"The Doc said about 2 more days if I keep my numbers up!"

"That's great. By the way, thanks for adding me to your friends and family list when you went into surgery. I would have been worried had I not known what was going on with you. I also added you to the prayer list at church."

"I thank you for adding me to the prayer list. God knows I need all the prayers I can get!

When they say I'm clear to socialize, I would like to attend church services with you.

I accepted Jesus as my Savior a long time ago, but I need to start fellowshipping again.

If the people there are anything like you, it must be an awesome bunch of believers!"

"I'm looking forward to that day!" Evelyn reached into her pocket and gave Tenitha an invitation card for the church she attends.

"I try to keep these on hand just in case someone needs prayer or someone to talk to. It has everything you need to know about my church. My shift starts in about 15 minutes, so I'll talk to you later. Take care."

Chapter Four

THE 2ND MEETING

As with everyone these days, life and work seems to keep us busy, we seem to loose touch with our friends and family.

Here it was, Sunday morning again, Evelyn's favorite day of the week. Wednesday was a close second. She walked into the church sanctuary, and there was Tenitha sitting in the back row.

"Oh, my goodness!!" Evelyn exclaimed. "It is so good to see you in the House of the Lord!"

As they embraced, Tenitha said, "I'm really blessed to finally be here!"

Evelyn guided Tenitha to the fourth row because she knew not to push her luck moving to the first or second row!

After service, Evelyn introduced Tenitha to several members, including the Pastor and his wife.

The last group of people she introduced was the group she has dinner with after church services, just about every Sunday.

"Everyone, this is Tenitha. Tenitha, this is Dala, her mom, Jaleese, and her fiancé, Darren.

We are having dinner at our favorite buffet. Would you like to join us?"

"That would be great!" Tenitha replied.

So, this gathering around the table was very exciting. Evelyn gave the quick version of how she met Dala, Jaleese, and Darren. Then Tenitha was inspired to tell everyone about the miracle that drew her and Evelyn together.

Evelyn felt her cup was overflowing on this first day of the week; great message at church service, great fellowship with good friends over a great meal. God is so good.

The next day, Evelyn gets a text from Tenitha asking for prayers.

She forwarded Tenitha's text to the prayer group and knew they would join her in prayer.

Evelyn tried calling Tenitha several times, but her calls went to voicemail.

Evelyn got to work extra early on Tuesday. She checked the list of new patients, and Tenitha's name was there.

Evelyn hurried to Tenitha's room and knocked softly before entering.

"Go away," Tenitha sobbed.

Evelyn came closer and noticed Tenitha's chart mentioned post op instructions for the nurses.

Knowing what this meant, Evelyn's heart ached for her friend.

"I guess I should have known good things don't last forever, " Tenitha said.

"Thanks for the prayers, but as you can see, I rejected my transplant, so they had to remove the kidney."

As Evelyn gently embraced Tenitha, she whispered a prayer and mourned with her friend.

"They're releasing me tomorrow, and I'll be going back to dialysis. My treatment days will be Monday, Wednesday, and Friday. I don't even know if I want to try a transplant again. This part is very disappointing."

"Well..." Evelyn started slowly, "I can understand if you don't want to try this again. I'm sure you know that a transplant is best with a live donor. I want to tell you a secret I've been holding. I had a test done to see if I'm a match to become your live donor. I came back to your room to tell you the good news, but you were already in surgery getting your transplant."

Tenitha began crying again. "Oh, my Lord. How He answers prayers!"

"I was just talking with God, telling Him I can't do this again unless it was with a live donor. Look at God!!"

With that, Evelyn called Tenitha's doctor and told him the situation.

Chapter Five

2ND SURGERY

They scheduled the transplant for the following morning. Evelyn took 2 weeks of personal time off and was approved for longer time off if needed.

All went well with the transplant. Evelyn was not expecting this kind of downtime, but it was for a good cause.

Three days later, Evelyn was packing up to go home. While thinking of everything that happened over the last week, in walks

Tenitha, "Wow, Evelyn, you look really good. No pain? They say it's worse for the donor."

"I'm feeling really good, a little sore, but I'm good! When do you get to go home?"

"Tomorrow. I would have been leaving today if this surgery wasn't too close to the removal of the kidney that failed."

Chapter Six

EPILOG

It's been 2 months, and Tenitha's transplant is really becoming her own. Instead of taking and trying more than a dozen pills to prevent rejection, she's down to 2 a day.

Sunday service was marvelous today. The message was about being thankful. Of course, Tenitha was very thankful. All during the service, she counted her many blessings, which caused tears to flow.

Hugging her gently, Evelyn asked Tenitha if everything was okay.

"Never better," she whispered. "This message today was my story. I've never been more thankful than right now."

They walked out of the sanctuary arm in arm and met with the others on their way to the buffet.

Tenitha proclaims to everyone, "God is so good!"

"All the time!!" was the reply in unison from this amazing group of believers.

LOOK FOR OTHER SHORT STORIES FROM EVELYN'S MOST AMAZING ENCOUNTERS

Flight 755

___

"Coming Soon"

"Evelyn's Most Amazing Encounter"

CONTACT THE AUTHOR

To contact the author for book speaking engagements, bulk purchases, or comments, please reach out to:

(E.L. Harden)

Email: elharden0054@live.com

www.ingramcontent.com/pod-product-compliance
Lightning Source LLC
Chambersburg PA
CBHW070036110426
42741CB00035B/2793